M257 Unit 5
UNDERGRADUATE COMPUTING

Putting Java to work

Packages and abstraction

Unit 5

This publication forms part of an Open University course M257 *Putting Java to work*. Details of this and other Open University courses can be obtained from the Student Registration and Enquiry Service, The Open University, PO Box 197, Milton Keynes MK7 6BJ, United Kingdom: tel. +44 (0)870 333 4340, email general-enquiries@open.ac.uk

Alternatively, you may visit the Open University website at http://www.open.ac.uk where you can learn more about the wide range of courses and packs offered at all levels by The Open University.

To purchase a selection of Open University course materials visit http://www.ouw.co.uk, or contact Open University Worldwide, Michael Young Building, Walton Hall, Milton Keynes MK7 6AA, United Kingdom for a brochure. tel. +44 (0)1908 858785; fax +44 (0)1908 858787; email ouwenq@open.ac.uk

The Open University
Walton Hall, Milton Keynes
MK7 6AA

First published 2007. Second edition 2008.

Edited, designed and typeset by The Open University.

Printed and bound in the United Kingdom by Hobbs the Printers Ltd.

ISBN 978 0 7492 6800 8

2.1

The paper used in this publication contains pulp sourced from forests independently certified to the Forest Stewardship Council® (FSC®) principles and criteria Chain of custody certification allows the pulp from these forests to be tracked to the end use (see www.fsc-uk.org).

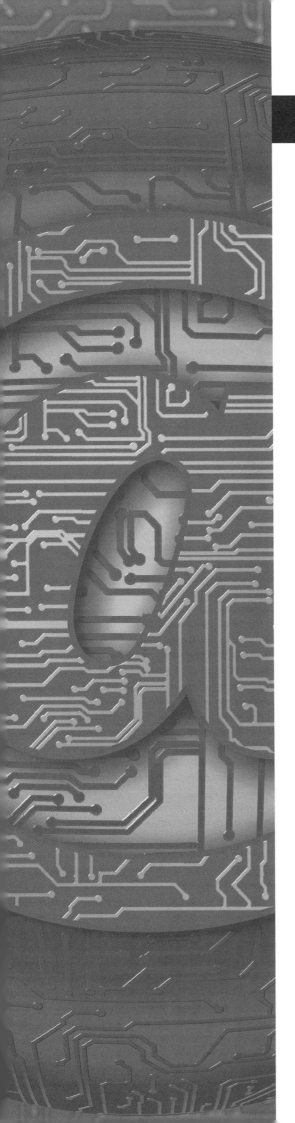

CONTENTS

Continued...

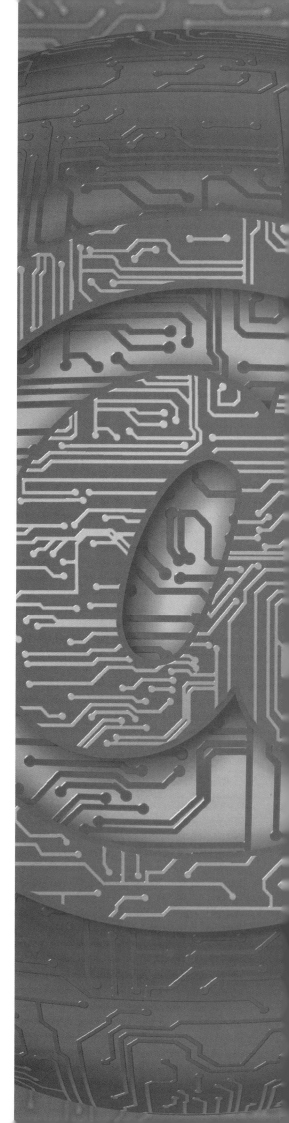

M257 COURSE TEAM

M257 *Putting Java to work* was adapted from M254 *Java everywhere*.

M254 was produced by the following team.

Martin Smith, Course Team Chair and Author

Anton Dil, Author

Brendan Quinn, Author

Janet Van der Linden, Academic Editor

Barbara Poniatowska, Course Manager

Ralph Greenwell, Course Manager

Alkis Stavrinides, External Assessor, Coventry University

Critical readers

Pauline Curtis, Associate Lecturer

David Knowles, Associate Lecturer

Robin Walker, Associate Lecturer

Richard Walker, Associate Lecturer

The M257 adaptation was produced by:

Darrel Ince, Course Team Chair and Author

Richard Walker, Consultant Author and Critical Reader

Matthew Nelson, Critical Reader

Barbara Poniatowska, Course Manager

Ralph Greenwell, Course Manager

Alkis Stavrinides, External Assessor, Coventry University

Media development staff

Andrew Seddon, Media Project Manager

Garry Hammond, Editor

Ian Blackham, Editor

Anna Edgley-Smith, Editor

Jenny Brown, Freelance Editor

Andrew Whitehead, Designer and Graphic Artist

Glen Derby, Designer

Phillip Howe, Compositor

Lisa Hale, Compositor

Thanks are due to the Desktop Publishing Unit of the Faculty of Mathematics and Computing.

1 Introduction

In this unit, we consider a number of facilities of Java that are particularly useful for structuring larger systems.

Classes and class hierarchies are the fundamental structuring concepts for Java programs. In larger programs, consisting of many classes, we often need a higher level of structure also. The Java language provides the concept of a **package** as a way to group a number of related classes. Large programs typically consist of a number of packages – this helps with management of the software development and maintenance processes.

Java contains a number of predefined packages, known as the **standard Java packages**. These form **libraries** of classes available for programmers to use. They provide a wide range of facilities including input/output, mathematical functions, graphical user interface components and data structures. A Java program normally has one or more packages of classes specially written for that application by the developer, together with classes from a number of standard Java packages.

We also explain two further concepts, interfaces and abstract classes, which are helpful in structuring hierarchies of related classes. **Interfaces** are a powerful way of specifying what a class should do, without specifying in detail how it should implement this. **Abstract classes** are useful in defining groups of classes related by inheritance.

In this unit, we aim to:

▶ enable you to use library classes from the standard Java packages and define your own packages for structuring large programs;

▶ explore some of the important collection classes provided within the `java.util` package;

▶ contrast the concepts of interfaces and abstract classes, and explain what each of these can be used for.

2 Java libraries

The standard packages, or **class libraries**, greatly extend the usefulness of the basic Java language, as the language core is actually quite minimal. They enable the programmer to create a wide variety of objects that implement much of the functionality required for typical Java applications.

Collectively, these libraries are sometimes called the Java **API** (application programming interface). The individual packages are also sometimes called APIs – for example, the `java.net` package may be referred to as the networking API.

In this section we discuss how we can make use of existing packages, and how to avoid problems that can arise when dealing with duplicate class names.

2.1 Accessing standard library classes

Table 1 shows the most important of the standard Java packages dealt with in this course. In this section we discuss how we can gain access to the classes defined in those packages, and in the next section we shall discuss how to find out more details of the classes in each package.

Table 1 Some packages from the Java class libraries

Package	Provides classes for
`java.applet`	programs (applets) that can be run from a web page
`java.awt`	Abstract Windowing Toolkit (AWT) – basic graphical user interface (GUI) components such as windows, fonts, colours, events, buttons and scroll bars
`java.io`	low-level input/output – for example, reading data from files or displaying on screen
`java.lang`	basic classes for the language – automatically imported and used by all Java programs
`java.net`	communication across a network, using clients, servers, sockets and URLs
`javax.swing`	creation of more sophisticated, platform-independent GUIs, building on the AWT capabilities
`java.util`	general utility classes, especially collection classes (data structures)

Each package contains a number of classes that the language designers knew would be useful in the intended application areas for Java. For example, the `java.net` package has a `URL` class that manipulates uniform resource locators (such as web page addresses). The **fully qualified name** of this class is its package name, `java.net`, followed by the separator (a dot), followed by the class name, `URL`, like this:

```
java.net.URL
```

To use this class in your program, you can refer to it by its fully qualified name. For example:

```
java.net.URL homeURL =
    new java.net.URL("http://www.open.ac.uk");
```

In Section 5, we shall explain the positioning of `import` statements more precisely.

This is obviously rather long-winded and a better approach is to write an **import** declaration near the start of your source file. You can then refer to the class by its **simple name**, URL, as follows:

```
...
import java.net.URL;
...
URL homeURL = new URL("http://www.open.ac.uk");
```

Note the compulsory semicolon terminating the `import` declaration. If you require other library classes, then separate import statements are needed. For example, if you require both the URL class and the `ArrayList` class from the `java.util` package then you should write:

```
import java.net.URL;
import java.util.ArrayList;
```

The `import` declaration informs the Java system which package to look in for details of any class it does not recognize from your source files alone. If you omit any necessary import statements, the compiler will indicate an error.

The asterisk character is a wild card.

If you require a number of classes within the same package then it is normally more convenient to use the **import-on-demand** facility, with a **wild card** instead of a specific class name, like the following:

```
import java.util.*;
```

This declaration allows the programmer to use any of the `public` items (mainly classes) contained in the `java.util` package. Using a wild card `import` declaration will not make your program any larger or slower than importing individual classes by name. Your compiled program will include only details of the classes you actually use, which is why this is referred to as import-on-demand.

2.2 | Class name clashes

Since import-on-demand seems to be both efficient and convenient, you may be wondering why there is a need for the alternative of importing specific named classes.

First, this can be useful as documentation when you want only one or two classes from a particular package – it makes it easier for someone reading the program to see where these classes come from.

More importantly, it can be helpful in case of a class **name clash** – two classes with the same name in different packages. For example, both the `java.util` package and the `java.sql` package have a class called Date. Suppose we have a program that uses the `java.sql` Date class and some other library classes from each package. What will happen if we write the following?

```
import java.util.*;
import java.sql.*;
...
Date d1 = new Date(DATE_IN); //Date is ambiguous
```

We get an ambiguous name, which causes a compilation error – the system cannot decide which Date class you want. You can get round this by always using the fully qualified name `java.sql.Date`, but this can be tedious.

For example, if you want only the `ArrayList` class from `java.util` but you want several classes from `java.sql`, you could define your imports as follows to avoid a clash:

```
import java.util.ArrayList;
import java.sql.*;
```

Perhaps more surprisingly, you can also write:

```
import java.util.*;
import java.sql.*;
import java.sql.Date;
```

This means that the `java.sql` definition of `Date` is used instead of the `java.util` definition. The specific import of the `Date` class hides (takes precedence over) any import-on-demand definition of the same name. This approach has the advantage that you can use any other classes from these two packages (as long as they do not have clashing names).

If you define and use your own class called `Date`, this will hide any `Date` class in packages you import using the import-on-demand facility.

If you need to use two classes from different packages with the same simple name, you will have to use the fully qualified class names throughout your program, as follows:

```
import java.util.*;
import java.sql.*;
...
java.sql.Date d1 = new java.sql.Date(DATE_IN);
java.util.Date d2 = new java.util.Date();
System.out.println("SQL date: " + d1.toString());
System.out.println("util date: " + d2.toString());
```

This resolution or avoidance of name clashes is an important reason for the use of packages. It is very useful for teams of programmers collaborating on development of large systems – different programmers can develop separate packages and may use some identical names for classes or other items specific to a package, without it causing a name clash.

2.3 The special case of `java.lang`

The only exception to this requirement for explicit naming of imported classes is the `java.lang` package. Since this package contains classes that every Java program will use, you do not need to include an `import` declaration for it – the Java system will automatically search it. In other words, the system automatically behaves as if every source file included the line:

```
import java.lang.*;
```

If you include this declaration anyway, it will not cause any problems – it will just be ignored.

3 The documentation of standard packages

Any Java system should contain API documentation, which describes each class in the standard packages. This documentation is normally in HTML format and hence you can examine it using a web browser. It is also freely available from the Sun Java website – in this case, you should ensure that you are accessing the correct version of the API for the development tools you are using.

Java is a rather sparse language in terms of what it can do. It gains its huge functionality from its packages – not only the standard packages that we have described above, but also the large number of special-purpose packages produced by commercial developers.

Because much of the functionality of Java is embedded in these libraries and they are too big for one person to remember, you will find yourself continually consulting the documentation. So it is often useful to keep open a window to the documentation while you are programming in Java.

3.1 What is in the API

The API provides a list of the standard packages, together with a brief description of the contents of each package (similar to Table 1, but with many more packages). This leads to details of each package, which include a list of all the classes and other items available for use by programmers. It is also possible to display this list as a class hierarchy.

For each class within the package, the API gives a description of the class with details of its public or protected attributes – its constructors, methods, variables, constants and so on. This information is in a standard format used for all classes and all packages and can be searched using an index.

3.2 JavaDoc

You may wish to look on the web for more information about this useful facility.

We have seen how the standard Java packages are documented and how essential this information is if you want to use any Java library classes. It is possible to provide the same sort of documentation for your own classes, using a standard tool called **JavaDoc** that is provided with the Java system. You need to place appropriately formatted comments in your source files and then supply these files to the JavaDoc program. This generates HTML files for your classes, in the same style as the API documentation.

This is particularly useful to those working in teams on large projects that may consist of many packages, in terms of communicating clearly what each package does. Because the documentation is generated automatically from the source files, it is also easier to keep it up to date than it would be using a manual approach.

4 The `java.util` package

Throughout this unit, we will focus our attention on one of the most useful and easy-to-understand libraries of classes: the Java utility package `java.util`. This package consists of a number of utility classes, which provide data structures and other facilities, including the following.

▶ The **Java Collections Framework**, first introduced with Java 2, is used for storing and managing objects of any Java type. It includes classes such as `LinkedList`, `ArrayList`, `HashSet`, `TreeSet`, `HashMap` and `TreeMap`. These names may sound a little strange and unfamiliar but together with some other useful concepts, such as iterators, they provide very useful and flexible functionality. We shall discuss them further in later sections.

▶ **'Legacy' collection classes** implement various simple data structures and were the only standard collection classes available in versions of Java prior to Java 2. These include the `Vector`, `Hashtable`, `Properties`, `Dictionary`, `Stack` and `BitSet` classes. We distinguish them here because in some ways they work a little differently to the Java 2 collection classes. They are widely used in older Java software, so it is useful to know about them. However, they are not recommended for use in new programs – you should use the Java 2 collection classes instead.

▶ The `Calendar` class and its subclass `GregorianCalendar` implement dates in a variety of representations.

▶ The `StringTokenizer` class is useful for processing text input.

▶ The `Random` class implements methods used for the generation of random numbers.

Activity 5.1
Exploring the API documentation.

The `StringTokenizer` class was discussed in *Unit 4*.

5 Creating your own packages

So far you have seen how packages are provided as part of the Java class library. It is perfectly possible for you to create your own packages, which is especially useful in organizing your work on large projects. A package forms a **compilation unit** – that is, a group of source files that you can compile independently of other parts of the system. Where a considerable number of classes are developed for a large system, this avoids having to continually compile and recompile the whole system as development proceeds.

Packages are also significant in terms of the visibility of items such as methods and instance variables. If these items are not explicitly declared as `private`, `public` and so on, they default to **package visibility** – that is, they are accessible to all classes in the same package.

To define a collection of classes as a package, you need to precede the source code of each of the classes with the keyword `package` followed by the name of the package, as follows:

```
package telNetCommsPackage;
```

Package names sometimes have several components, separated by a dot, to reflect the hierarchical organization of packages. For example:

```
package general.utilities;
package javax.swing;
```

Each component of the package name typically corresponds to a subdirectory within the base directory for this project or the base directory for Java libraries, as appropriate. The example later in this section explains this in more detail.

However, this correspondence between package name and directory structure is not mandated by the language specification and may vary between different Java systems.

Relationships can be defined between groups of packages. Packages can have **subpackages**. For example, `java.awt` has many subpackages such as `java.awt.event` and `java.awt.image`. However, the term subpackage may be a little misleading. Each of these three packages contains a number of classes and other items useful for building basic GUIs. The important point is that their contents are distinct from one another. For example, `java.awt` does not contain `java.awt.event`; if you want classes from both of these packages then you must explicitly import from both, as follows:

```
import java.awt.*;
import java.awt.event.*;
```

The subpackages of `java.awt` are named in this way to make clear that they depend on `java.awt`.

If you omit a package declaration, the Java system will assume your classes are in an 'unnamed package', which typically consists of all the Java source files residing in the current directory for Java source files. This works well enough for small, experimental programs, but larger programs should be explicitly structured into packages to benefit from the advantages outlined above.

How to refer to the classes in a package

If the class you want is in the same package as the class you are working on, then you use the simple name of the class you want, as normal. If the class is in a different package – whether it is one written by you or by someone else in your team, or it is in a standard Java package – you use the `import` facility, as discussed in Section 2.

Consider Figure 1, which shows the structure of a file directory for a project. A project will typically have a top-level directory (or folder) with a number of subdirectories and possibly several levels of subdirectories for a complex project. We assume here the commonly used approach whereby the Java system expects to find each package in a separate subdirectory, with the subdirectory having the same name as the package.

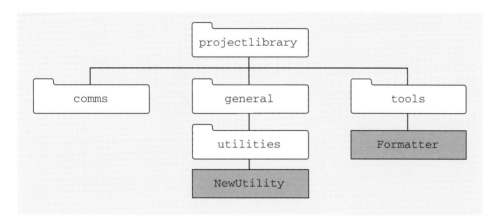

Figure 1   A directory structure for class files in a software project (class files shown shaded)

If we have grouped a number of classes in a package defined as:

```
package tools;
```

then these classes will be stored in the `tools` subdirectory of the top-level directory `projectlibrary`. When we want to import one of the classes in this package, say the `Formatter` class, we use:

```
import tools.*;
```

or:

```
import tools.Formatter;
```

In large projects, we may wish to arrange a package to have a number of subpackages. Suppose we have grouped a number of utility classes in a subpackage defined as:

```
package general.utilities;
```

In this case, the classes must be in the `utilities` subdirectory of the `general` directory, as shown in Figure 1. So the components of a package name are separated by dots and each component corresponds to a subdirectory, starting from the top-level directory for the project.

Let us focus on the `NewUtility.class` file, which contains the compiled code (bytecode) for a class that we want to use. If we wanted to use the class contained in the file `NewUtility.class` that is contained in the directory `utilities`, which in turn is held in the directory `general` that forms part of the top-level directory `projectlibrary`, then we would write:

```
import general.utilities.NewUtility;
```

To have access to any class in this package we can use the import-on-demand style:

```
import general.utilities.*;
```

Activity 5.2
Creating your own project
and package.

The `import` declarations in a source file are placed immediately after the `package` declaration, if any.

SAQ 1

Referring to the system in Figure 1, assume the directory `comms` has a subdirectory `TCPcomms`, which in turn has a subdirectory `lowlevel`. The class file `UsefulStuff.class` is stored in the package in the `lowlevel` directory. How can the class `UsefulStuff` be accessed by code in another package of this system?

ANSWER...

The `import` statement needs to list the packages and subpackages corresponding to the directory structure. So we would need the following:

```
import comms.TCPcomms.lowlevel.UsefulStuff;
```

Note that the class name `UsefulStuff` is used without the suffix `.class`, which all Java bytecode files have. Alternatively, we could use import-on-demand:

```
import comms.TCPcomms.lowlevel.*;
```

Finally, of course, we could omit the `import` declaration and use the fully qualified name for the class throughout our program.

6 Two simple collection classes

A **collection** is an object that can be used for storing, retrieving and manipulating groups of items. These items may be primitive data or objects. If you have studied other computer languages, you may be familiar with broadly the same idea under a different name, such as container class or data structure class.

Collections typically represent data items that form a natural group, like a mail folder (a collection of letters), the icons in a screen window, or a telephone directory (a collection of name-to-phone-number mappings).

Homogeneous collections store data that is all of the same type – for example, an array of `int` can store only `int` values. **Heterogeneous collections** may contain data of a variety of types.

This requires some more advanced concepts such as abstract classes and interfaces, which we shall explain in later sections.

The aim of this section is to examine two relatively simple collection classes from the Java Collections Framework, `ArrayList` and `HashMap`, and introduce some general concepts that apply to most collections. Later in this unit, we shall discuss the Java Collections Framework in more detail.

The `ArrayList` class is a more flexible alternative to arrays. Objects of class `HashMap` can store pairs of linked items in key–value pairs and allow efficient retrieval of the value associated with a given key. The `ArrayList` and `HashMap` classes should be used instead of the `Vector` and `Hashtable` classes, respectively – the latter were widely used in older Java code.

6.1 Generic classes

A generic class has at least one member of an unspecified type. A programmer must then specify the desired type when creating an instance of the class.

Java collections in version 1.5 are generic, and so it is normal to provide a type when creating an instance. The instantiation then behaves as if it had been written to operate on the provided type.

The type(s) you provide on instantiation appear in the API as single letters in angle brackets after the name of the class, e.g. `ArrayList<E>`. The `<E>` is known as a formal type parameter, and when creating the collection you should supply an actual type for it.

6.2 The `ArrayList` class

Objects of the generic class `ArrayList` have some similarity to arrays – they can store a number of references and the data can be accessed via an index. An `ArrayList` can automatically increase in capacity as necessary, unlike an array, which is of a fixed capacity once it has been declared. The `ArrayList` object requests more space from the Java run-time system, if necessary.

We need to define two important terms in connection with `ArrayList` objects. The **capacity** of an `ArrayList` object is the maximum number of items it can currently hold (without being extended). The **size** of an `ArrayList` object is the current number of items stored in the `ArrayList`, which clearly cannot exceed the current capacity.

The `ArrayList` class has a number of constructors. For example:

```
final int INIT_CAPACITY = 100;
//zero-argument constructor
ArrayList<String> list1 = new ArrayList<String>();
//one-argument constructor
ArrayList<Date> list2 = new ArrayList<Date>(INIT_CAPACITY);
```

The angle brackets can be read as 'of', for example ArrayList of Strings.

The `ArrayList` constructor with no arguments sets up an empty `ArrayList`, which is then referenced by `list1`. The initial capacity is set to a default value. The `ArrayList` capacity is expanded automatically as needed when items are added.

The second constructor with one argument can be used to specify the initial capacity – in this case 100 elements. This can be more efficient in avoiding repeated work by the system in extending the list, if you know approximately the required initial capacity. Normally, it is best to allow the system to manage the capacity of the `ArrayList` as required. Any attempt to access the unused part of an `ArrayList` object will generate an exception.

The first declaration of an `ArrayList` specifies that it will hold `String` references while the second specifies that `Date` references will be stored.

While an `ArrayList` represents an advance over the use of an array, it is not ideal in its use of memory. As soon as an `ArrayList` requires more space than its current capacity, the system will allocate more memory space for it. The details of this depend on the implementation of the Java library but, in general, the extension is more than required for the items about to be added. So there will often be empty locations within an `ArrayList` – that is, the *size* will often be less than the *capacity*. This means that it can be a slightly inefficient solution to the problem of storing variable amounts of data.

There are a large number of methods associated with `ArrayList` objects. Table 2 shows the basic methods for operations such as adding, removing, retrieving and updating items. You can look up the full details in the API documentation.

There are two overloaded `add` methods and two overloaded `remove` methods – recall that overloaded methods have the same name but different numbers or types of arguments. One of the `add`/`remove` pairs allows adding and removing at a particular index, similar to an array. The other pair behaves more like a **list**, adding an item to the end of the `ArrayList` and removing an object from anywhere in the list if it matches the specified object.

Table 2   Basic methods of the `ArrayList<E>` class

Method signature	Description
`void add(int index, E el)`	inserts `el` at the position indicated by `index`
`boolean add(E el)`	adds `el` to the end of the `ArrayList`, increasing its size by one
`Iterator <E> iterator()`	returns an iterator over the elements in this `ArrayList` in proper sequence
`E get(int index)`	returns the element at the specified position in this `ArrayList`
`boolean remove(Object obj)`	removes the first occurrence, if any, of the specified element in this `ArrayList`
`E remove(int index)`	removes the element at the specified position in this `ArrayList` and returns its reference
`E set(int index, E el)`	replaces the element at the specified position in this `ArrayList` with the specified element, returning a reference to the removed element

`E` is the type the programme specifies on instantiation, and defaults to `Object` if not supplied.

The concept of an iterator will be explained in Subsection 8.2.

Table 3 shows standard utility methods of `ArrayList` – these utility methods occur in most collection classes.

Table 3   Standard utility methods of the `ArrayList` class

Method signature	Description
`boolean equals(Object obj)`	compares the specified object with this `ArrayList` for equality
`boolean isEmpty()`	tests if this `ArrayList` has no elements
`int size()`	returns the number of elements in this `ArrayList`
`boolean contains(Object obj)`	tests if the specified object is an element in this `ArrayList`

Some methods operate on `Object` for generality and backward compatibility.

There are some general points to note. The `add` methods 'make room' within the `ArrayList` object by moving items along and renumbering the indexes, if necessary. The `remove` methods 'close up any gap' created by the deletion of an item and renumber the indexes, if necessary. The `set` method simply overwrites the existing reference, so there is no need to change any indexes and the total size of the `ArrayList` object is unchanged.

An example of the use of the `add` method is shown below:

```
ArrayList<User> list = new ArrayList<User>();
User u = new User("John");
list.add(u);
```

Removing items is straightforward. For example, the code:

```
User u2 = list.remove(0);
```

will remove the user object stored at position 0 in the list.

When using methods that search the `ArrayList` for a matching object, like the `remove` method listed in Table 2 or the `contains` method listed in Table 3, you must ensure that the class for the stored data has a suitable `equals` method – see the next section for details.

SAQ 2

How many different methods are there for removing an individual item from an `ArrayList` and what is the difference between them? You may need to consult the API documentation for details.

ANSWER ....

From Table 2 above, there are two overloaded versions of `remove`:

```
E remove(int index)
```

This removes the element at the specified index in the list and closes the gap (renumbers the index for any subsequent elements). It also returns a reference to the removed element. This is useful if you know the index in the list for this element, but not its contents.

```
boolean remove(Object obj)
```

This removes the first element that matches the specified object and closes the gap (renumbers the index for any subsequent elements). Clearly this method is useful when you already know the details of the object to be removed, but not its index. It returns `true` or `false` depending on whether a matching element was found in the `ArrayList`.

By the way, you cannot tell from Tables 2 and 3 but there is also a third way (!), which uses the iterator returned by the `iterator` method listed in Table 2 – this will be explained later in Subsection 7.2.

6.3 The use of `equals`

There are various ways of searching for a particular object in a collection. The class `ArrayList`, for example, has the method `contains`, which returns a `boolean` value to indicate whether a matching object was found. For this to work properly, any class whose objects are being stored in the `ArrayList` (such as the `User` class) must have an **equals** method declared as follows:

```
public boolean equals(Object obj)
```

Note that the argument to the `equals` method must be of type `Object`, not of the same type as the class being tested for equality. This is because it is important to ensure that this `equals` method *overrides* the default implementation of `equals` that all classes would inherit from the `Object` class.

Library classes in Java will normally have an `equals` method already defined.

6.4 An example of using the `ArrayList` class

We now develop some code based on an `ArrayList` in order to give you an idea of the power of the class library.

We construct a data structure that contains the details of a computer, together with all the computers to which it is connected in a local network.

The first part of the class, which describes the linkage, is shown below:

```
class LinkingInfo
{
    private String computer;
    private ArrayList<String> linkedComputers;
    ...
}
```

The string `computer` contains the name of the computer whose details are documented by this class. The `ArrayList` referenced by `linkedComputers` contains the names of the computers that are linked to that computer.

We will assume that a number of methods are required. These are specified below.

▶ `String getComputerName()` returns the name of the computer whose details are in this object.

▶ `int getNumberOfLinks()` returns the number of computers that are linked to the first computer.

▶ `boolean isLinked(String comp1)` returns `true` if the computer `comp1` is linked to the computer documented by this object; otherwise it returns `false`.

▶ `void addComputer(String comp1)` adds the name of computer `comp1` to the list of linked computers. If the computer is already in the list of linked computers, then a `ComputerErrorException` exception is raised with the message 'Computer already in links'.

▶ `void removeComputer(String comp1)` removes the computer named `comp1` from the linked computers. If the computer is not in the list of linked computers, then a `ComputerErrorException` exception is raised with the message 'Computer not in links'.

We assume for now that `ComputerErrorException` has been defined elsewhere. Recall that raising an exception is not the preferred way of detecting predictable error situations, like those above that could give rise to the exception `ComputerErrorException`. Programs should check beforehand, using the method `isLinked`, to avoid causing an exception when adding or removing computers from the linked computers.

See *Unit 4*, Subsection 9.2 for a discussion of exceptions and how to deal with predictable errors.

We shall define two constructors. The first is provided with the name of the computer for which the linking information is to be held and an initial value of the number of locations to hold linked computers. The second has a single argument, the name of the computer, and uses the default initial capacity. The code for these two constructors is shown below:

```
public LinkingInfo (String computerName, int capacity)
{
    linkedComputers = new ArrayList<String>(capacity);
    computer = computerName;
}
```

```
public LinkingInfo (String computerName)
{
    linkedComputers = new ArrayList<String>();
    computer = computerName;
}
```

We now need to develop some of the methods. The code for the first two methods is shown below. Method `getComputerName` is trivial as it merely returns the name of the computer.

```
public String getComputerName ()
{
    return computer;
}

public int getNumberOfLinks ()
{
    return linkedComputers.size();
}
```

Activity 5.3
Completing the coding of the `LinkingInfo` class.

The `getNumberOfLinks` method returns the number of linked computers. This uses the `size` method, which returns the number of items in an `ArrayList`. This is why we did not need an instance variable for the `LinkingInfo` class to record the number of computers that are linked.

6.5 | Object wrapper classes

In some (so-called pure) object-oriented languages everything is an object, including the equivalents of the primitive data types in Java – integers, characters, floating-point numbers, and so on. In Java, mainly for efficiency reasons, the language designers decided to treat primitive data types in the way we have explained: that is, they store actual values.

To bridge this gap, Java 1.4 employed **object wrappers**, which 'wrap around' or encapsulate all the primitive data types and allow them to be treated as objects. There is an object wrapper class for each primitive data type, as summarized in Table 4. Note that the class names are not entirely consistent – the compiler will remind you if you get mixed up!

Table 4   Object wrapper classes

Primitive type	Object wrapper class
int	Integer
long	Long
short	Short
byte	Byte
float	Float
double	Double
char	Character
boolean	Boolean
void	Void

The object wrapper for `int` is the class `Integer`. It contains constructors for creating an `Integer` object from an `int` or from a `String`. It also has methods to return the value of the `Integer` object as a `String`, as an `int`, or as various other primitive data types such as `float` or `short`. So, for example, you could have a collection:

```
ArrayList<Integer>intlist = new ArrayList<Integer>();
```

In Java 1.4 we would have written:

```
intlist.add(new Integer(3));
```

In Java 1.5 we can deposit `Integer` objects directly into a collection and also remove them directly. For example, the code below places the `Integer` 3 into an `ArrayList` object, retrieves it, then adds 2 to it and displays the result (5):

```
ArrayList <Integer> holder =
            new ArrayList <Integer>();
holder.add(3);
System.out.println(holder.remove(0)+2);
```

An interesting part of this code is the final line where we retrieve the `Integer` that was stored and then add 2 to it. This seems an incorrect thing to do since, with the exception of the + operator that is used to concatenate strings, operators such as *, -, ++ can be applied only to basic types such as `int`.

What actually happens in the final line is that the code:

```
holder.remove(0)
```

returns an `Integer` object, which is then automatically converted to an `int` and the + operator applied. The process of converting an object wrapper to its corresponding primitive type is known as **unboxing**, and was introduced in Java 1.5.

Another example of unboxing is shown below, this time using the `Character` object wrapper:

```
ArrayList <Character> holder =
            new ArrayList <Character>();
holder.add('Z');
System.out.println("The answer is "+ holder.remove(0));
```

Here the character `'Z'` is retrieved and then concatenated with the string `"The answer is "`; the result is then displayed as:

```
The answer is Z
```

From Java 1.5, it is no longer necessary to manually wrap primitives, as we now have **autoboxing**, which does this for us.

Collections such as the `ArrayList` collection can be sequentially accessed via a special type of for statement known as the `for-each` statement. This iterates over the objects contained in a collection and extracts each of them. An example of this statement in action is shown below.

```
ArrayList <Character> holder =
            new ArrayList <Character>();
holder.add('a');
holder.add('b');
holder.add('c');
for (Character i : holder)
        System.out.println("The value is "+ i);
```

Here three characters are added to the `ArrayList` object `holder`. The for statement then iterates, extracting out each of the stored `Character` objects, unboxes them and concatenates them with the string `"The value is"` before displaying the concatenated string that is formed. The general form of this `for` statement is:

```
for (Classname element_identifier: collection_identifier)
```

The *Classname* gives the type of the stored object, *element_identifier* is given the values of the object and *collection_identifier* identifies the collection that is traversed. An example is shown below:

```
for(Employees empl: empColl)
{
    ...
    if (empl.pay()>100000)
    {
        System.out.println(empl);
    }
}
```

Here the collection `empColl` that contains employee objects is traversed, and each element retrieved and assigned to the variable `empl`. Each `empl` then invokes `pay()`, which extracts the annual salary of the employee. This is then compared with 100000 and any employee who earns more than a hundred thousand pounds is displayed.

We have shown you how the `ArrayList` class can store references and wrapped primitives. We have also emphasized the importance of using the Java API documentation. Next, we describe another important Java collection class, namely `HashMap`.

6.6 The `HashMap` class

In many applications we require two types of object to be associated with each other. Some examples are as follows.

▶ Staff in a large company need to be associated with internal telephone numbers.

▶ A network may need to maintain a link between each user's logon id and their current password and other details, such as access rights and allowable storage space.

▶ Members of staff in a personnel system will need to be associated with details such as their tax details, salary and home address.

A hash table represents a simple version of the relational tables used in modern database systems.

A **hash table** can store pairs of linked items in **key–value pairs**. In this generic collection, the programmer must specify the type of both the key and the value to instantiate the collection; for example, `<String, Integer>`. In the first example above, the key could be the name of the staff member and the value would be their telephone number. The main characteristic of a hash table is that it allows efficient retrieval of the value associated with a given key. The keys must be distinct: that is, no two keys can be identical. The values need not be distinct – for example, two people could share the same telephone number.

Figure 2 shows a logical view of this type of association, using the example of named computer users and their (encrypted) passwords. Here the keys are the users' names. The name is used to retrieve the value of the password efficiently.

Key (user's name)	Value (password)
A Einstein	Ahjgeteu
N Mandela	Khaiwncoiw
L Van Beethoven	nu8we92
E Peron	LAmdA3hx
Z Mao	hwn3jh8kp
R Tagore	Slheynvsa
E Dickinson	BjKtQhPy7K

Figure 2   A logical view of a **HashMap** object

The hash table concept is implemented in Java by means of the `java.util` class `HashMap`. This association of keys with values is known as a **map** – we say it maps keys to values. The `HashMap` is a particular way of implementing such a map and this should be used in preference to the older `Hashtable` class.

There are a number of constructors associated with `HashMap`. For example, we can create a collection mapping strings to strings as follows:

```
final int INIT_CAPACITY = 100;
HashMap<String,String> table1 = new HashMap<String,String>();
HashMap<String,String> table2 = new HashMap<String,String>
                                (INIT_CAPACITY);
```

The `HashMap` constructor with no arguments sets up an empty `HashMap`, which is then referenced by `table1`. The initial capacity is set to a default value. The `HashMap` capacity is expanded automatically as needed when items are added. The details of how hash tables work are beyond the scope of this course.

The second constructor with one argument is used to specify the initial capacity – in this case 100 'slots' for key–value pairs. This can be efficient in avoiding repeated work by the system in extending the hash table, if you know approximately the required initial capacity. If you are not familiar with how hash tables work, it is best to use the simpler constructor, with a default initial capacity.

Notice the text `<String,String>`; this indicates that the key part is a string and the value part is also a string.

An example of a `HashMap` in action is shown below. It declares a `HashMap` `hm` that has `String` keys and values. Three pairs of key–value data are added to `hm` and the value associated with the key `"Darrel"` is retrieved and displayed. After this a `for` statement is used to retrieve each key and its associated value; these are then displayed.

```
HashMap <String,String> hm = new HashMap<String, String>();
System.out.println("Hello there");
hm.put("Dave", "London");
hm.put("Robert", "Sheffield");
hm.put("Darrel", "Milton Keynes");
System.out.println("Darrel is associated with "+hm.get("Darrel"));
for(String name: hm.keySet())
{
    System.out.println
        (name+" is associated with the city "+hm.get(name));
}
```

The code `hm.keySet` returns the collection of keys associated with `hm`.

Table 5 shows some of the basic methods for data manipulation associated with the `HashMap` class. `V` is the value type and `K` is the key type that the collection has been instantiated for. If no types are specified then they default to `Object`.

Table 5   Basic methods of the `HashMap` class

Method signature	Description
`V get(Object key)`	returns the value to which the key is mapped in this hash map
`V put(K key, V value)`	maps the key to the specified value in this hash map, creating a new key–value pair if necessary
`V remove(Object key)`	removes the key and corresponding value from this hash map

Note that the `put` method updates the value corresponding to an existing key in the table. However, if the key is not already in the table, it creates a new key–value pair.

Table 6 shows that `HashMap` has a similar set of standard utility methods to those for `ArrayList` (see Table 3). However, note that the `contains` method in Table 3 is replaced by two separate methods in Table 6, which check for either a matching key or a matching value.

Table 6   Standard utility methods of the `HashMap` class

Again, some methods operate an `Object` for generality and backward compatibility with pre-1.5 collection.

Method signature	Description
`boolean equals(Object obj)`	compares the specified object with this hash map for equality
`boolean isEmpty()`	returns true if this map contains no key–value mappings
`int size()`	returns the number of items (key–value pairs) in this map
`boolean containsValue(Object value)`	tests if some key maps into the specified value in this hash map
`boolean containsKey(Object key)`	tests if the specified object is a key in this hash map

The rest of this section outlines the use of such a hash map in a simple example. This application involves mapping user names to the computer that they use – both items are of type `String`.

The class skeleton for this is shown below:

```java
import java.util.HashMap;
class UserComputers
{
    private HashMap<String,String> userTable;

    public UserComputers (int capacity)
    {
        /* constructor creates a hash map,
        'capacity' specifies its initial capacity */
    }

    public void addLink (String userName, String computerName)
    {
        /* adds the information that user userName is
        associated with computer computerName */
    }

    public String getComputer (String userName)
    {
        /* returns the name of the computer that userName is
        associated with */
    }

    public boolean isThereAUser (String userName)
    {
        /* returns true if there is a user
        userName, false otherwise */
    }

    public boolean isThereAComputer (String computerName)
    {
        /* returns true if there is a computer computerName,
        false otherwise */
    }

} // end class
```

Activity 5.4
Providing the code for the
class UserComputers.

Providing the detailed code for this class is left as an activity.

7   Interfaces

A key idea in object-orientation is that objects have a public external behaviour together with a hidden implementation – the details of how the object works. This ensures that software systems can be built from interacting collections of objects, without each object depending on the detailed implementation of the other objects. In Java, as in most object-oriented languages, the external behaviour of an object is typically defined by its constructors and public methods.

7.1   The `Comparable` interface

Java has a specific construct called an interface, which is very useful in large systems in defining the behaviour required from a class. As a first attempt, you can think of an interface as being like a class with method headers, but nothing else – no method code, no instance variables, and so on. It specifies what a class should do without defining how the class should do it. Here is an example from the Java libraries:

T is the type being compared, which defaults to `Object`.

```
public interface Comparable<T>
{
    int compareTo(T o);
}
```

The `Comparable` interface is useful when we want to compare objects or put them into some sort of order. A method like `compareTo` without any method body is known as an **abstract method**. All methods in an interface are automatically `public` (and abstract), so there is no need to write the word `public` in the method header within the interface. An interface can have more than one method. It can also define constants, but not variables. Any constants in an interface are implicitly defined as `public static final`, so they need not be declared as such. For example:

```
public interface RGBColours
{
    int RED = 1;
    int GREEN = 2;
    int BLUE = 3;
    void showColour(int colour);
}
```

The Java interface concept is different from the idea of user interfaces. Programming of graphical user interfaces will be explained in *Unit 7*.

Something a bit like a class but with only abstract methods or constants is clearly not of much use by itself. To make use of an interface we need a class to **implement** the interface. The class does this by providing the code for any abstract methods in the interface.

So any class that implements the `Comparable` interface must have a method called `compareTo` for the specified type `T`. The interface declaration specifies how to invoke the `compareTo` method and that it returns an `int`, but this is not enough. We also need something that specifies the meaning of the `compareTo` method – that is, what it is to do. The method should compare two objects and return an indication of which is, in some appropriate sense, the larger. Consider the following method call:

```
int result = x.compareTo(y);
```

This should set the value of `result` to zero if `x` and `y` are equal, some positive value if `x` is larger than `y` or a negative value if `x` is smaller than `y`.

A class can indicate that it conforms to a particular interface by using the keyword `implements` in the class header. For example:

```
class Employee implements Comparable <Employee>
{
    private String name;
    private String address;
    private float salary;
    ...
}
```

The `Employee` class must provide a complete `compareTo` method, as well as its other methods. This allows the class to define an appropriate measure of comparison. For example, suppose we want to use this to rank employees by salary. We could then write the `compareTo` method as follows (note that the `public` modifier is required here, as it will not be implicit):

```
public int compareTo (Employee otherEmployee)
{
    if (salary > otherEmployee.salary) return 1;
    if (salary < otherEmployee.salary) return -1;
    return 0;
}
```

Note that here we have used two `if` statements, instead of an `if`, `else-if`, `else` construct. Since a `return` statement will effectively bring the method invocation to a halt, the effect here is the same. That is, if it reaches the first `return` statement, the method will stop and there is no chance that it can 'fall through' to the next `if` statement or the final `return` statement.

How can we use this newly 'comparable' `Employee` class? Java has a special class in `java.util` called `Arrays`. This offers a number of very useful operations that can be applied to arrays of objects. For example, there is a static method called `sort`, which can be used to arrange the objects of an array in order ... but only if they implement the `Comparable` interface (so they have a `compareTo` method). So, for example, to sort an array of `Employee` objects into salary order, we could write:

```
Employee [] staff = new Employee [STAFF_COUNT];
...
Arrays.sort(staff);
```

This enables the `sort` method to be general purpose – it knows how to sort any type of object, as long as each object has a `compareTo` method. Incidentally, it is not good enough for an object to implement its own `compareTo` method without declaring that it conforms to the `Comparable` interface. The Java compiler must be able to check at compile time that the objects being sorted have a `compareTo` method.

SAQ 3

Say whether each of the following interface definitions is valid or invalid and state your reason.

(a)
```
public interface FriendlyInterface
{
    void displayHello()
    {
        System.out.println("Hello");
    }
}
```

(b)
```
public interface UnfriendlyInterface {}
```

(c)
```
public interface FixedInterface
{
    int MAX_WORD = 200;
}
```

(d)
```
public interface Textable1
{
    final int MAX_WORD = 200;
    String text;
    void displayText();
}
```

(e)
```
public interface Textable2
{
    boolean displayText(int maxWords);
}
```

ANSWER...

(a) Invalid – because it contains a concrete method.

(b) Valid – although perhaps not very useful.

(c) Valid – this defines a constant as the modifiers `public static final` are implicitly applied.

(d) Invalid – because `text` is either an attempt at an instance variable or is an uninitialized constant.

(e) Valid – this defines a single method, which is implicitly defined as `public abstract`.

7.2 The `Iterator` interface

We have seen that a Java interface is not a class – it cannot be instantiated. You can, however, declare variables of an interface type. Any class that implements the interface may be referenced by such a variable. So, using the example from the previous section, the following is possible:

```
Comparable<Employee>employee1 = new Employee(...);
```

To show how a variable of an interface type can be used, we consider the `Iterator` interface. This allows you to traverse (or 'iterate' through) any collection, such as an `ArrayList`, without needing to know details of its implementation. Table 7 lists the three methods for the `Iterator` interface.

Table 7 Abstract methods of the `Iterator` interface

Method signature	Description
boolean hasNext()	returns true if the iteration has more elements
E next()	returns the next element in the iteration
void remove()	removes from the underlying collection the last element returned by the iterator (optional operation)

`E` is the type the interface is implemented for.

You can access each element of a collection in turn by repeatedly invoking the `next` method. You use the `hasNext` method to check if there are any more elements to iterate through.

Most collection classes in Java have an associated iterator – an object that implements the `Iterator` interface for their type. Table 2 described the `iterator` method for the `ArrayList` class – this returns a reference to an object that implements the `Iterator` interface. We can use it to display the items in an `ArrayList`, as follows:

```
ArrayList<String> userList = new ArrayList<String>();
...
Iterator <String>listIt = userList.iterator();
System.out.print("The list is [");
while (listIt.hasNext())
{
    System.out.print(listIt.next() + " ");
}
System.out.println("] ");
```

To help understand this code, let us look at a specific example. Suppose that the `ArrayList` object `userList` contains the user IDs of four users. We represent this diagrammatically as in Figure 3, for simplicity ignoring the fact that the `ArrayList` actually stores references rather than the strings themselves.

Figure 3   A logical view of an **ArrayList** object containing four user ID strings

Table 8 shows the result of executing the above code for each iteration of the `while` loop. The second and third columns show the values returned by the iterator methods `hasNext` and `next` during each iteration – strictly speaking, the `next` method returns an object reference, rather than the characters themselves.

Table 8   Trace of iteration

Iteration	Result from listIt.hasNext()	Result from listIt.next()
1	true	"ab3"
2	true	"pj4"
3	true	"rd1"
4	true	"db4"
5	false	

The loop terminates after the test at the beginning of the fifth iteration. The final printed output from this would be as follows:

```
The list is [ab3 pj4 rd1 db4]
```

In this example, `listIt` is a variable of the interface type `Iterator`. It can reference any object that implements the `Iterator` interface. Hence, almost exactly the same code can be applied to any collection that provides an iterator. To use a different type of list, the linked list, we would need to change only the first line of the above example, as follows:

```
LinkedList<String> userList = new LinkedList<String>();
...
```

Alternatively, we could use yet another type of collection, which implements the mathematical concept of a set, simply by changing the first line to this:

```
HashSet<String> userList = new HashSet<String>();
...
```

See Section 11 for more on the `LinkedList` and `HashSet` classes, which are part of the Java Collections Framework.

Note that we can regard iterators as disposable. Once we have completed the traversal of a collection, using an iterator, we no longer need the iterator object and it can be made available for garbage collection by the system. If we need to traverse a collection again later, it is normally best to obtain a new iterator object.

You might be tempted to ask: why are you teaching us `Iterator` objects? After all, the `for-each` statement will do the same thing. In general, this is correct: if you are just going to traverse a collection then use the `for-each` statement. However, if you need to remove items from a collection then you'll need to use an `Iterator` object and, in particular, the method `remove`. This deletes from the collection the item returned by the most recent call to `next`. This is the preferred approach when you need to remove a number of data items from most collections because it is normally more efficient.

For example, if we have an `ArrayList` object containing details of users, we can use an iterator to find and remove all users whose department is 'Sales':

```
ArrayList<User> userList = new ArrayList<User>();
...
// add various User items to the list
...
Iterator<User> listIt = userList.iterator();
while (listIt.hasNext())

{
    User user = listIt.next();
    String userDept = user.getDept();
    if (userDept.equals("Sales"))
    {
        listIt.remove();
    }
}
```

It is important to ensure that each call to `remove` is preceded by a call to `next`.

We could have done this selective deletion with the `ArrayList` methods we have previously seen, such as the method in Table 2, declared as:

```
boolean remove(Object obj)
```

However, this would be much less efficient as it scans the list, looking for a matching item, scanning from the start of the list every time. Incidentally, the iterator `remove` method is the third way of removing items from an `ArrayList`.

Activity 5.5
Using an interface.

<h2>7.3   Interfaces and inheritance</h2>

Some programming languages permit a class to inherit from two or more other classes – this is known as **multiple inheritance**. In Java, this is not permitted – a Java class can inherit from at most one other class, using the `extends` keyword. Typically, multiple inheritance is used when a programmer wants a class to inherit certain behaviour from each of a number of superclasses. This can, however, lead to a number of complications, such as making the class hierarchy rather complex.

Java neatly avoids such problems by the use of interfaces. Classes can implement more than one interface, as well as potentially extending one class – this gives an alternative to multiple inheritance, without most of its complications. For example, consider the following class header:

```
class MonthlyEmployee extends Employee
    implements Comparable, Serializable
{
    ...
}
```

If the class implements more than one interface, the interface names are listed in any order, separated by commas.

Although an interface is not a class, it is possible for an interface to inherit from another interface, using the `extends` keyword. For example:

```
public interface List extends Collection
{
    ...
}
```

This means that the `List` interface has all the methods or constants defined in the `Collection` interface and may add more methods or constants to this. Interfaces can have an inheritance hierarchy, similar to a class hierarchy. For example:

```
public interface Set extends Collection
{
    ...
}
public interface SortedSet extends Set
{
    ...
}
```

In fact, multiple inheritance is allowed for interfaces (unlike for Java classes). This is consistent with permitting classes to implement more than one interface. For example:

```
public interface PersistentComparable
    extends Comparable, Serializable
{
    ...
}
```

SAQ 4

Assume `Employee` and `Parent` are classes; `Comparable` and `Serializable` are standard Java interfaces. Are these declarations valid? If not, why not?

(a) `class MonthlyEmployee extends Employee, Parent`
    `implements Comparable`

(b) `class MonthlyEmployee extends Comparable`

(c) `class MonthlyEmployee extends Employee implements Parent`

(d) `class MonthlyEmployee implements Comparable, Serializable`

(e) `public interface Sortable extends Comparable`

(f) `public interface Sortable extends Parent`

(g) `Comparable employee1 = new Comparable();`

ANSWER...

(a) Invalid – a class cannot inherit from more than one superclass.

(b) Invalid – a class cannot extend an interface, although it can implement it.

(c) Invalid – a class cannot implement another class: we cannot get multiple inheritance this way!

(d) Valid – a class can implement more than one interface.

(e) Valid – an interface can inherit from another interface.

(f) Invalid – an interface cannot inherit from a class.

(g) Invalid – you can define a variable (like `employee1`) of an interface type but you cannot create an object of an interface type.

We have seen a number of examples of the uses of interfaces in Java. They play an important role in many other parts of the language and its packages. We shall consider this in later units when we discuss threads (which allow programs to do more than one thing at a time) and graphical user interfaces (GUIs). Later in this unit, we shall see that interfaces are also an essential part of the Java Collections Framework.

8 Abstraction in class hierarchies

It is in the nature of any class hierarchy that as you move through the classes from the top to the bottom of the hierarchy, the classes that you encounter become more and more specialized versions of the classes that lie above. Or, turning this around – moving from the bottom towards the top of the hierarchy, the classes become more and more general and abstract. At some point in this process, the top-level classes become so general that it may be more useful to consider them as part of the structure of the hierarchy than as classes from which we would want to create objects. This is the motivation for abstract classes.

As an example, consider Figure 4, which illustrates classes in a database used for a personnel application.

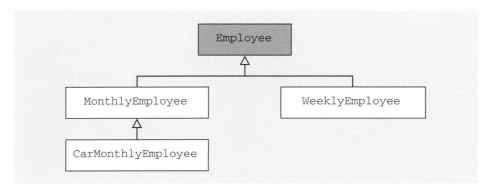

Figure 4   An example of a class hierarchy with an abstract class (shaded)

The top class `Employee` contains information required for all the employees in an organization: it will, for example, contain instance variables for the name of an employee, their address and their tax details. This class has two more specialized subclasses. The first class, `MonthlyEmployee`, represents those employees who are paid monthly and who often will receive special payments such as travelling expenses and commissions. The other class, `WeeklyEmployee`, represents other workers who are paid weekly and whose pay is calculated in a different way from monthly paid employees – for example, they may receive overtime payments.

At the lowest level of the hierarchy is the even more specialized class `CarMonthlyEmployee` for monthly paid staff who are provided with a car by the company. These would be staff such as sales staff for whom car travel is essential. Inside this class there would be methods and instance variables specific to this variation from its parent class. For example, there would be an instance variable describing the make of car and methods to retrieve and set this variable.

The classes in the hierarchy in Figure 4 represent an increasingly more specialized view of the notion of an employee. The topmost class represents the most general concept of an employee; this contains instance variables and methods common to all employees. As you proceed down the hierarchy, the category of employee becomes more specialized, with additional data or functions, or different ways of carrying out similar functions. It is likely that no real employee will correspond to the `Employee` class and, in practice, only objects corresponding to the subclasses of `Employee` will be created. We can take this one step further and define `Employee` in such a way that `Employee` objects cannot be created – this is the idea of an *abstract class*.

9 Abstract methods and abstract classes

In this section we discuss how the idea of abstraction in a class hierarchy can be implemented using Java.

9.1 An example of an abstract class – Employee

An abstract class is declared using the keyword `abstract`. For example:

```
public abstract class Employee
{
    ...
}
```

Such a class cannot be instantiated: that is, you cannot create an `Employee` object.

Abstract classes normally have at least one abstract method. An abstract method has a header, but has no implementing code associated with the header. The implementation code must be supplied by subclasses of the abstract class. The keyword `abstract` is also used to identify these methods. Note the difference from interfaces, which have abstract methods but do not require the word `abstract` in the declaration.

For example, we can define an abstract method named `calculatePay` within the `Employee` class, as follows:

```
public abstract int calculatePay ();
```

As before, we use the semicolon to indicate that no code is provided for the abstract method `calculatePay`. This method will be inherited by all subclasses of `Employee`.

SAQ 5

What would be the effect of this attempt to declare the abstract method `calculatePay` using empty curly brackets, and why?

```
public abstract int calculatePay (){}
```

ANSWER...

Even empty curly brackets constitute an implementation for this method – although a method that does nothing is not a very useful implementation! This contradicts the declaration of the method as `abstract` and causes a compilation error. To correct the compilation error, we would need either to remove the `abstract` keyword or to replace the curly brackets with a semicolon.

Concrete classes and methods

A fully implemented class, with no abstract methods, is known as a **concrete class**. We also use the term **concrete method** to identify fully implemented methods, as opposed to abstract methods. It is possible for an abstract class to have one or more other abstract classes as subclasses. However, at some point in the class hierarchy the subclasses must be concrete to allow objects to be created. In our example, only `Employee` is abstract – all the other classes are concrete. There is no Java keyword to declare concrete classes – classes are assumed to be concrete unless they are defined as abstract.

The code for `calculatePay` must be provided by any concrete class that inherits from `Employee`. For example, the `MonthlyEmployee` class can be defined as follows:

```
public class MonthlyEmployee extends Employee
{
    // new instance variables for MonthlyEmployee
    // constructors for MonthlyEmployee
    // any new methods for MonthlyEmployee

       . . .
    public int calculatePay ()
    {
        // code which calculates the
        // pay of a monthly employee
    }
    . . .
}
```

The important point about abstract classes with abstract methods is that they place requirements on their concrete subclasses to implement certain methods. You must follow these requirements because you cannot create an object of an abstract class. However, as we shall see later, we *can* define a variable of an abstract class type and this is often useful.

The `MouseAdapter` class will be explained in *Unit 7*.

Finally, in this section, we note that it is permissible for an abstract class to have no abstract methods and possibly a number of concrete methods. There are some useful examples of this in the Java standard packages, including the adapter classes, such as `MouseAdapter`.

When you should not use an abstract class

A class type should be declared `abstract` only if the intent is that concrete subclasses can be created to complete the implementation. If you simply want to prevent creation of objects of a particular class, the proper way to express this is as follows: declare a constructor of no arguments, make it `private`, never invoke it, and declare no other constructors.

A class of this form usually contains class-wide methods and variables. The class `java.lang.Math` is an example of a class that cannot be instantiated. It is used only to provide various mathematical functions and constants, for example:

```
double length = Math.sqrt(AreaOfSquare);
```

It does not make sense to create objects of type `Math`, as they would not have any stored data. So, its declaration is as follows:

```
public final class Math

{

    private Math(){} // constructor never used

    ... class-wide methods and variables

    ...

}
```

9.2 Designing an abstract class hierarchy

It is worth looking at another example, as abstraction is an important principle in object-oriented design. This time we consider how to construct an abstract class hierarchy by **factoring out common behaviour** in a number of subclasses.

The example concerns an information system for a warehouse, perhaps for an e-commerce company. The system needs to keep track of a wide variety of items that customers may wish to order. We can define a number of classes to model the various sorts of items, such as `Book`, `MusicCD`, `VideoDVD`, `ComputerGame`, `HouseholdItem`, `GardenItem` and so on. We assume that a detailed object-oriented analysis and initial design has been carried out to identify the required classes and the details of each class – its data items and behaviour. As a result, we find that there are certain common features between many of the classes. For example, each item has a name, an item code and a unit price. Each class will need instance variables, `itemName`, `itemCode` and `unitPrice`, and associated methods for accessing or modifying this data, such as `getUnitPrice` and `setUnitPrice`. Instead of repeatedly implementing these separately in each class, we can *factor out* the common behaviour by defining a more general class `Item`, from which all these classes inherit. The `Item` class will define instance variables `itemName`, `itemCode` and `unitPrice`. The associated methods for accessing or modifying this data may be either concrete or abstract, depending on the circumstances; for example, `getName` is likely to be the same for all subclasses of `Item`, so it can be implemented as a concrete method. If returning the unit price depends on factors that differ between types of item, then `getUnitPrice` could be left as an abstract method to be overridden by each specialized subclass. In this case, `Item` must be declared as an abstract class.

We can apply this factoring at a number of levels, if appropriate. So, for example, we may be able to identify commonality between `MusicCD`, `VideoDVD` and `ComputerGame`. In this case we can factor out the common aspects and define a superclass, say, `MultimediaItem`. This could be either concrete or abstract, as before, depending on how similar the common behaviour is.

Figure 5 shows a possible hierarchy for this.

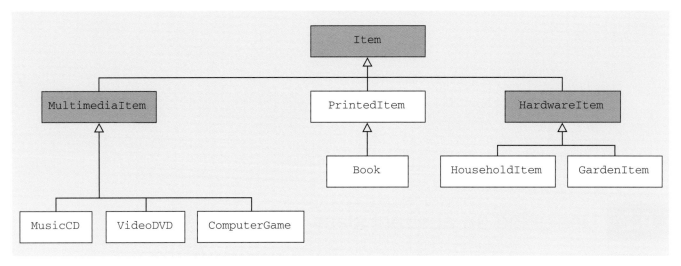

Figure 5   Inheritance hierarchy for e-commerce items, showing abstract classes (shaded)

Here are some code fragments to illustrate how some of the various classes could be declared:

```
public abstract class Item
{
    private String itemName;
    private String itemCode;
    protected int unitPrice;

    public String getItemName ()
    {
        . . .
    }

    public abstract int getUnitPrice ();
    . . .
} // end class Item

public abstract class MultimediaItem extends Item
{
    . . .
}

public class MusicCD extends MultimediaItem
{
    . . .
    public int getUnitPrice ()
    {
        // concrete method, so code goes here
    }
}
```

```
public class VideoDVD extends MultimediaItem
{
    ...
    public int getUnitPrice ()
    {
        // concrete method, so code goes here
    }
}

public class PrintedItem extends Item
{
    ...
    public int getUnitPrice ()
    {
        // concrete method, so code goes here
    }
}

public class Book extends PrintedItem
{
    ...
    /* need not implement getUnitPrice()
    because inherits it from PrintedItem
    but could still override it if need be */
}
```

9.3 Abstract classes and polymorphism

You may be thinking that all this abstract class definition is rather a lot of trouble for not much reward. So in this section we present an example to show how it can be useful.

An inheritance hierarchy consists of a group of related classes, which by definition have some similarities (related by inheritance) and some differences (otherwise we would need only one class). We can take advantage of these similarities to write software that is extensible in certain ways, without extensive modification.

Consider the personnel example in Section 9. Suppose we have stored details of many employees of different categories in an array. But what type should the array be? If we define an array of `MonthlyEmployee` we cannot store `WeeklyEmployee` objects in it, and so on. Therefore we must declare an array of the highest type in the hierarchy, namely `Employee`:

```
Employee staff [] = new Employee [MAX_EMPLOYEES];
```

Since we are not creating `Employee` objects, only `Employee` references, this is all right. We can then store references to objects of any subclass of `Employee` in the array.

Remember that a subclass reference can always be assigned to a variable declared as being of a superclass type. The opposite assignment is not possible – a superclass reference cannot be directly assigned to a variable declared as being of a subclass type – but it may be possible to do this by using a cast.

SAQ 6

Explain why we cannot store `WeeklyEmployee` references in an array declared as follows:

```
MonthlyEmployee staff[] =   new MonthlyEmployee[MAX];
```

ANSWER...

Because it requires assignments like the following to work:

```
staff[0] = new WeeklyEmployee(...);
```

In general, you cannot assign a reference to a variable of a different type. The left-hand side is a variable of type `MonthlyEmployee` and the right-hand side is a reference to a `WeeklyEmployee` object. If this were allowed, then the system would treat the object as if it had all the methods of a `MonthlyEmployee` object and, in general, this is not the case. It would only be allowed if `WeeklyEmployee` were a subclass of `MonthlyEmployee`.

We can now take advantage of the common behaviour imposed on the hierarchy of classes by the `Employee` abstract class. If we want to display the wages for all employees we can proceed as follows:

```
public void displayPayroll ()
{
    for (int e = 0; e < staff.length; e++)
    {
        int pay = staff[e].calculatePay();
        String name = staff[e].getName();
        System.out.println(name + " " + pay);
    }
}
```

Here we are using the `calculatePay` method, which we know every employee object must have regardless of whether it is a `MonthlyEmployee` object, a `CarMonthlyEmployee` object or any other subclass of `Employee`. This is an example of **polymorphism**.

We say that the method invocation for `calculatePay` is polymorphic because Java executes the version of the `calculatePay` method appropriate to the object type. For `MonthlyEmployee` objects it uses the `calculatePay` method defined in that class, for `CarMonthlyEmployee` objects it uses the `calculatePay` method defined in that class, which overrides the `calculatePay` method in its superclass, and so on.

The `getName` method invocation may not be polymorphic because this is defined in the `Employee` class and so is the same for all subclasses, unless it has been overridden.

So where is the payoff? Suppose we want to extend the `Employee` class hierarchy by introducing new classes for junior employees still in training, where we need to store various special details, such as the employees' training programmes. We might need to have `WeeklyTrainee` and `MonthlyTrainee` classes that are subclasses of `WeeklyEmployee` and `MonthlyEmployee` respectively.

If we define these two new classes in this way, the payoff is that we do not have to change any parts of the code that use polymorphism, such as the `displayPayroll` method above. This will work for all types of employees, including the new ones, without any change to the source code – although we do, of course, have to recompile the program. This extensibility is very helpful in limiting the effect of changes to existing software.

Activity 5.6
E-commerce class hierarchy with abstract classes.

SAQ 7

Figure 6 shows an extension of the class hierarchy of Figure 4. It adds the new classes `WeeklyTrainee` and `MonthlyTrainee` as subclasses of `WeeklyEmployee` and `MonthlyEmployee` respectively.

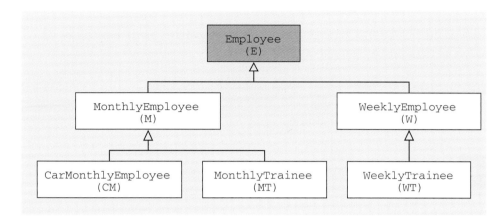

Figure 6 Extension of class hierarchy from Figure 5, showing abbreviations for class names as used in SAQ 7

Recall that both the `WeeklyEmployee` and `MonthlyEmployee` classes contain an implementation of the abstract method `calculatePay` defined in the `Employee` class. We have also seen that the `CarMonthlyEmployee` class overrides the `calculatePay` method to reflect differences in the pay calculation for employees of this type.

Considering the two newly defined classes in Figure 6, `MonthlyTrainee` overrides the `calculatePay` method (with a different implementation) whereas `WeeklyTrainee` does not.

Suppose we have an array of various kinds of employee objects, declared as at the start of this section:

    Employee staff[] = new Employee[MAX_EMPLOYEES];

If this contains a sequence of objects of the following classes (with the obvious abbreviations for class names, as shown in Figure 6):

M	M	WT	CM	WT	W	MT

which versions of the `calculatePay` method will be invoked on this data by the `displayPayroll` method shown above?

ANSWER...

Each class will invoke its own implementation of `calculatePay` if it has one. If not, it uses a version inherited from its superclass. The compilation process will have ensured that each concrete class has a concrete `calculatePay` method available. So the versions in the following classes are used:

M	M	W	CM	W	W	MT

10 Relationships between classes and objects

We have now encountered a number of ways in which classes and objects can be related or may depend on each other, including inheritance, abstract classes and interfaces. In this section we compare these various approaches and give some guidelines as to their key features and when they should be used. We also discuss the important idea of object composition, which we have already used but not explicitly named.

10.1 Abstract classes compared to interfaces

In this section we summarize the differences and similarities between abstract classes and interfaces.

The differences between an interface and an abstract class in Java

Interface:

▶ An interface is not a class.

▶ All its methods are abstract and, apart from its abstract methods, it may contain only constants. The methods are implicitly treated as `abstract` and the constants are treated as if declared as `public static final`.

▶ An interface can be implemented by any number of unrelated classes, which declare this using the `implements` keyword. A class may implement any number of interfaces.

Abstract class:

▶ An abstract class uses the keyword `abstract` in the class header.

▶ It normally has at least one abstract method, either defined within the class or inherited from a superclass, and its abstract methods must be explicitly declared `abstract`. It can also have concrete methods (that is, it may be fully implemented) and instance variables, unlike an interface.

▶ It can only constrain its own concrete subclasses, by requiring them to implement its abstract methods – it cannot constrain any other classes.

The similarities between an interface and an abstract class in Java

▶ They can both place requirements on objects of other classes.

▶ Both can have abstract methods (although neither need have abstract methods).

▶ You cannot create objects of an abstract class type or an interface type. You can, however, create reference variables of either type. These are normally used to refer to an object of a subclass of the abstract type or to an object of a class that implements the interface, respectively.

▶ Both can inherit: the abstract class from another class; the interface only from another interface.

10.2 Inheritance compared to composition

We have seen how inheritance between classes can be useful. It helps in designing groups of classes that model relationships between objects in the problem domain. It can also facilitate code reuse and extension of code – for example, via polymorphism, as shown in the previous section. Abstract classes can often be helpful in both these aspects of inheritance – in designing class hierarchies and in allowing polymorphism and code reuse.

However, it is important not to get carried away with the power of inheritance. In the right situation, it is very useful, but sometimes other forms of relationship between classes are appropriate. One such relationship is **composition**, also known as **aggregation**. This occurs when objects of a class contain objects of another class – an object of the class is 'composed' of objects from one or more other classes.

In fact, we have seen many examples of object composition already, but we did not give a name to this relationship. For example, the `Date` class, representing details of the `Date` desert fruit, could be defined as follows:

```
public class Date
{
    private String botanicalName;
    private String areaOfOrigin;
    private ArrayList knownDiseases;
    ...
}
```

So a `Date` object is composed of two `String` objects, an `ArrayList` object and possibly other objects. In Java, the `Date` object actually holds references to the `String` objects and the `ArrayList` object, as shown in Figure 7, rather than holding the object data directly. However, this does not affect the key point – this is an example of composition, not inheritance.

There is a further level of composition in this example – the `ArrayList` object referenced by `knownDiseases` must contain references to other objects, perhaps strings or more complex objects. For simplicity, we omit this further level from Figure 7, but it is useful to note that in general there can be several levels of composition like this.

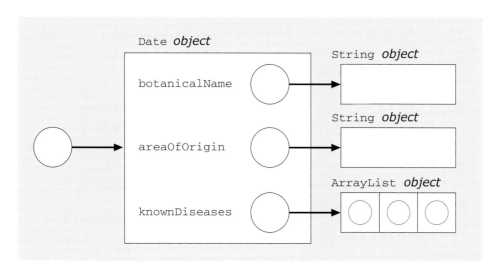

Figure 7   A **Date** object is composed of **String** objects and an **ArrayList** object

This is sometimes explained by saying that the `Date` object *has* two `String` objects and *has* an `ArrayList` object. We call this the **has-a** relationship by contrast with class inheritance, which is sometimes called the **is-a** relationship. Note also that composition is defined as a relationship between *objects*. Inheritance is normally explained as a relationship between *classes*, although this clearly implies a relationship between objects of those related classes.

Using the example in Figure 4, a `MonthlyEmployee` is a kind of `Employee` and a `CarMonthlyEmployee` is a kind of `MonthlyEmployee`. It would not make sense to define an inheritance relationship between `Date` and `ArrayList`, for example. We cannot sensibly say that a `Date` is a kind of `ArrayList`. We could perhaps define a superclass of `Date`, perhaps an abstract class called `Fruit`, to represent the common attributes of various fruits such as dates, figs and olives – then it makes sense to say a `Date` is-a `Fruit`, as shown in Figure 8.

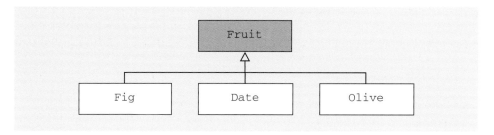

Figure 8   Class inheritance relationship: a **Date** is-a **Fruit**

10.3 Choosing between composition and inheritance

Most object-oriented systems will require a mixture of composition and inheritance. The choice of which one to use is sometimes obvious, but can in some cases be a difficult decision, involving weighing up advantages and disadvantages. Experienced object-oriented designers and programmers get a feel for this issue, but there are a few useful guidelines and these are as follows.

▶ You can use inheritance if there is a clear is-a relationship between the two classes – that normally means that one is a more specialized version of the other.

▶ Do not use inheritance just to reuse code, if there is no sensible is-a relationship. If you ignore this, you may find that the subclass inherits some data or methods that are not necessary and may be inappropriate.

▶ Do not use inheritance just to make use of polymorphism, if there is no sensible is-a relationship. In this case, you can normally use an interface to achieve polymorphism.

▶ Use composition if the has-a relationship clearly applies – objects of the class need to make use of the facilities offered by objects of another class.

▶ Composition tends to be more flexible than an inheritance relationship – an inheritance relationship is quite fragile, in that any coding changes to the public methods of a superclass can also affect any code using its subclasses.

▶ Inheritance hierarchies can be easier for readers of your code to follow than a network of composition relationships – this is not a reason to prefer one over the other, but something to be aware of.

▶ In general, both inheritance and composition will be needed, but one would expect composition to be more common.

More on collection classes

You have already seen some of the simpler Java collection classes, such as the `ArrayList` class. The aim of this section is to look in more detail at the grandly titled *Java Collections Framework*, which was introduced in the Java 2 version of the language. The framework classes are in the `java.util` package.

This framework makes use of some of the more advanced features of Java, which we have considered recently – in particular, *interfaces* and *abstract classes*. The guiding principle in this is to separate interface from implementation. The framework uses interfaces to define the facilities offered by various collection classes. It offers one or more implementations of these interfaces, but leaves open the possibility of adding further implementations at a later date, perhaps to take advantage of some aspect of a specific application.

You can use many of the classes from the framework without understanding their underlying structure, detailed in the next subsection. However, the framework is an excellent illustration of the power and flexibility of Java interfaces and is worth studying for that alone.

11.1 The structure of the Java Collections Framework

The basic structure of the framework is defined by a number of interfaces, as shown in Figure 9. The most important of these are the `Collection` and the `Map` interfaces. The distinction is clear if we look at the method offered by each interface for adding an item to the relevant collection class.

The `Collection` interface specifies the method:

```
boolean add(E el);
```

where `E` is the type the interface is implemented for. This can be used by most of the 'classic' data structures, such as arrays, lists, stacks or sets, and the framework offers implementations for some of these.

The `Map` interface specifies the insertion method:

```
V put(K key, V value);
```

where `K` and `V` are the key and value types. Classes that implement `Map` deal with key–value pairs in the same way as we saw with hash tables earlier. Values are retrieved from a map by supplying the key to the `get` method, which is defined as follows:

```
V get(Object key);
```

Although interfaces are not classes, as we have seen, it is possible for an interface to inherit from another interface. The Java 2 Collections Framework defines a hierarchy of interfaces, most of which are shown in Figure 9.

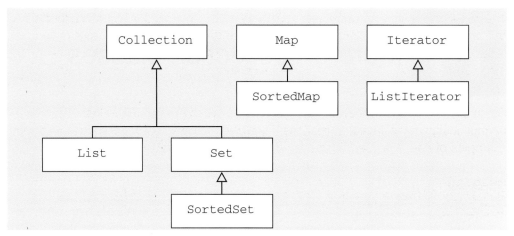

Figure 9   Inheritance hierarchy of interfaces in the Java 2 Collections Framework

This shows that there are interfaces to define the operations for lists, sets and maps, and more specialized interfaces for sorted sets and sorted maps, which as the name suggests can return their data in some appropriate ordering. The `Iterator` interface and its more specialized subinterface `ListIterator` are powerful tools for traversing the various collections in a consistent way, without the need to know the implementation details of each collection.

The implementation of the interfaces is handled by another hierarchy – this time the hierarchy of collection classes, shown in Figure 10.

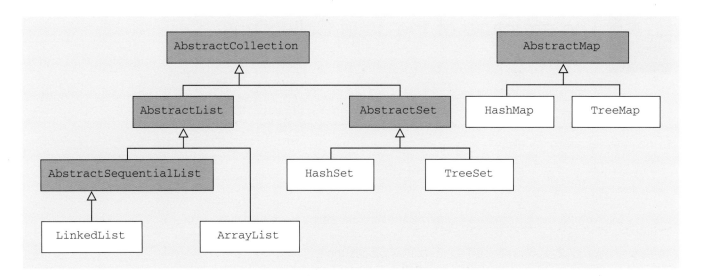

Figure 10   Class hierarchy in the Java 2 Collections Framework (abstract classes are shown shaded)

Figure 10 shows six concrete classes that inherit from the five abstract classes, which are shown shaded. This shows that the abstract concept of a set, for example, as defined by interface `Set` and partially implemented by abstract class `AbstractSet`, can be finally implemented in one of two ways – a `HashSet` (using a hash table as the underlying data structure) or a `TreeSet` (using a tree as the underlying data structure). Similarly there are two possible implementations for lists (using an array approach or a linked list) and two ways of implementing maps (with hash table or tree options, similar to sets). A **tree** is a sort of data structure widely used in computer science. For this course, all you need to know is that trees are particularly useful for efficient storage and retrieval of data in a particular sorted order.

The framework makes it possible for you (or the language designers or some third party) to add other implementations, if none of the standard implementations suits your requirements. As long as you stay within the framework specified by the interfaces and the abstract classes, any new implementation should require little or no change to code that previously used another implementation.

So much for how the framework is organized. There is much more to learn about the careful design of the Java 2 Collections Framework, but we now move on to look at some examples of how it is used. This should be much more straightforward.

11.2 The `LinkedList` collection class

This collection implements a list using the **linked list** approach. Each data item in the list is linked to the adjacent data items by storing a reference to those items. There is also a link from each data item to the previous data item. This is a dynamic collection, in that space is created for items as they are added to the list, so there is no limit to the size of such a list (unless the system runs out of memory completely).

Figure 11 shows a representation of how items are stored in a linked list. The circles represent references to list items, so each list component contains both data and a reference to the next list component. The data items themselves must be objects, so in fact they are also references but, for clarity, we do not show this in Figure 11. The items `head` and `tail` shown are variables that store references to the first and last items in the list respectively.

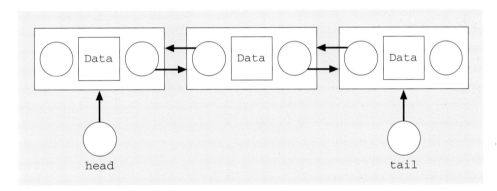

Figure 11   A linked list storing three data items

The basic `add` operation for this collection class places the new item at the end of the list, so it becomes the last item. In Figure 12, the new data item is shown with diagonal hatching. The references stored by the old last item and by the `tail` variable are updated to refer to this new item. So linked lists are extensible data structures, but unlike `ArrayLists`, they use only as much memory as they need for their current data items.

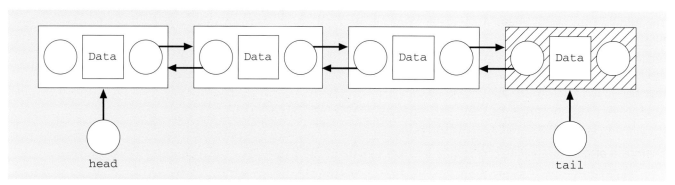

Figure 12   The list after adding a new item (shown hatched)

The class LinkedList offers a wide range of methods, enabling it to be used to implement a number of other standard data structures, such as stacks and queues. Table 9 lists some of the more important methods of this class.

Table 9   Some methods of the LinkedList class

Method signature	Description
boolean add(E el)	appends the specified element to the end of the list
void add(int index, E el)	inserts the specified element at the specified position in the list
boolean contains (Object obj)	returns true if the list contains the specified element
E get(int index)	returns the element at the specified position in the list
Iterator<E> iterator()	returns an iterator over the elements in the list (in proper sequence)
E remove (int index)	removes the element at the specified position in the list
boolean remove (Object o)	removes the first occurrence of the specified element in the list
E set(int index, E element)	replaces the element at the specified position in the list with the specified element
int size()	returns the number of elements in the list

Note the two overloaded add methods – recall that *overloaded* methods have the same name but a different signature because the number or types of their arguments are different. The first of these methods always adds to the end of the list. The other allows you to specify the index position where the new item is inserted – the list index starts at 0, the same as for Java arrays and ArrayList objects.

Similarly there are two remove methods, one specifying an index position, and the get and set methods, for accessing and updating list items, also specify an index position.

This choice of methods is typical of the Java Collections Framework – all lists (collections that implement the `List` interface) must offer these methods, but in most implementations some of the methods may be relatively inefficient. In the case of the `LinkedList` class, the methods that operate at a specified index are typically rather inefficient, since they must start at the head of the list and follow through all the linking references. A better way if you want to process a number of list items is to use an `Iterator`, as explained in the next subsection.

There are also 'convenience methods' particular to the `LinkedList` class, such as `getFirst`, `getLast`, `addFirst`, `addLast`, `removeFirst` and `removeLast`. These are 'convenience methods' in that we could easily program them in other ways, but they are convenient for these commonly required operations.

SAQ 8

How could the convenience methods mentioned above be programmed using other, more basic, `LinkedList` methods from Table 9? Assume that `numList` references a `LinkedList` object that contains enough items so that all the methods work properly and that `item` is a reference to a suitable object for adding to or removal from the list.

ANSWER..

```
    getFirst    :   item = numList.get(0);
    getLast     :   item = numList.get(numList.size() - 1);
    addFirst    :   numList.add(0,item);
    addLast     :   numList.add(item);
or alternatively,
                    numList.add(numList.size(), item);
    removeFirst :   item = numList.remove(0);
    removeLast  :   item = numList.remove(numList.size() - 1);
```

Traditionally, computer science courses teach you how to program your own list classes. The Java collection classes take all the hard work out of this and offer a choice of correct and efficient implementations. The example below shows some of the `LinkedList` methods in action:

```java
// construct an initially empty list
LinkedList<Integer> numList = new LinkedList<Integer>();

numList.add(99);
numList.add(103);
numList.add(88);

// there are now three items in the list
System.out.println("First item is " + numList.getFirst());
System.out.println("Last item is " + numList.getLast());
System.out.println("Item at index 1 is " + numList.get(1));
```

Activity 5.7
Using a `LinkedList`.

The list operations also allow linked lists to be used as a stack, a queue, or a double-ended queue (a **deque**). Hence there is no need for special classes for these structures. The 'convenience methods' mentioned above come in handy here. For example, stacks can use the list operations `addFirst`, `getFirst` and `removeFirst`; queues can use `addLast`, `getFirst` and `removeFirst`; and double-ended queues can offer all of these operations.

SAQ 9

What output would you expect from the above example code for `LinkedList`?

ANSWER...

Since the `add` method adds items to the end of the list, it should contain items in the order 99, 103, 88 when all three have been added. Hence printing the first and then the last item displays 99 then 88. The item at index 1, retrieved by the `get(1)` method, is the second item in the list, since the index starts from the front of the list at index 0. This value is 103. So the output is as follows:

```
First item is 99
Last item is 88
Item at index 1 is 103
```

11.3 The `HashSet` collection class

Sometimes you want to store data in such a way that you do not care in which order it is stored, but you do want to be able to find it again quickly. Arrays and lists maintain data in a certain order, and if you do not know exactly where the data is then searching for it can be rather slow. The hash table, and its Java implementation by class `HashMap`, which we discussed earlier, is just right for this sort of application.

The mathematical idea of a set is a collection of unique items, with operations to add and remove items and to test whether a given item is in the set. In this case, *unique items* means that the set holds no duplicate items.

The class `HashSet` is a particular implementation of the set concept. It implements the `Set` interface, making use of the same underlying mechanisms found in the `HashMap` class for adding and quickly retrieving items (in fact, it uses a `HashMap` object). This is useful because the order of items in a set is not important, only the fact that these items are present (or members of the set, in mathematical terms). Table 10 (overleaf) summarizes some of the methods of the `HashSet` class.

Table 10 Some methods of the `HashSet` class

Method signature	Description
`boolean add(E el)`	adds the specified element to the set, if it is not already present
`void clear()`	removes all of the elements from the set
`boolean contains(Object el)`	returns true if the set contains the specified element – that is, it tests for set membership
`boolean isEmpty()`	returns true if the set contains no elements
`Iterator<E> iterator()`	returns an iterator over the elements in the set
`boolean remove(Object el)`	removes the given element from the set, if it is present, and returns true if the element was present
`int size()`	returns the number of elements in the set (its cardinality)

The example code below illustrates simple use of the methods of the `HashSet` class:

Activity 5.8
Using the `Set` interface.

```
// create a new set with no members
// note use of variable of interface type 'Set'
Set<Integer> s = new HashSet<Integer>();
if (s.isEmpty())
{
    System.out.println("Set initially empty");
}

s.add(23);
s.add(25);
s.add(11);
// three integers added

System.out.println("The set has " + s.size() + " elements");
s.remove(23);
// there are now only two integers in the set
System.out.println("The set now has " + s.size() +
                   "elements");

if (s.contains(25))
{
    System.out.println("25 is in the set");
}

s.clear(); // delete all items from the set
if (s.contains(25))
{
    System.out.println("Something wrong!");
}
```

11.4 Other collection classes

There are two collection classes within the Java Collections Framework illustrated in Figure 10 that are based on the data structure known as a tree.Trees provide an efficient structure for storing and retrieving data in some specified order. For this course, you do not need to know the details of how trees work but they are explained in many standard books on data structures. Some brief details of these two classes, `TreeMap` and `TreeSet`, are listed below. Consult the API documentation if you require further details.

▶ `TreeMap` is an alternative implementation for maps. It is based on the tree data structure and has the useful property that the data is sorted in key order, unlike a `HashMap`, which guarantees no particular order for traversal of its data. It implements the interface `SortedMap`, which inherits from the `Map` interface.

▶ `TreeSet` has been briefly mentioned earlier. We revisit it here simply to point out that it gives an implementation of a set class that allows access to the set items in sorted order – that is, it is a sorted set that implements the `SortedSet` interface. As with the `TreeMap` class, it is based on the tree data structure.

The class `Collections`, also in the `java.util` package, is not strictly a collection class, despite its name. It is a special class with only static methods and provides a range of **algorithms** that can be applied to various collection classes. So, for example, it has methods for sorting, searching, reversing and randomizing items in `Lists` and arrays and for such things as finding the maximum or minimum value of most types of collections.

Activity 5.9
Developing a word-frequency counter using a `List` and a `HashMap`.

Requirements for classes to be held in a collection

We have discussed how collection classes work and pointed out, in passing, some of the requirements for the classes of objects to be held in collections. For example, we saw in Subsection 6.1 that objects stored in an `ArrayList` must have a properly defined `equals` method for the `Arraylist.contains` method to work.

There are a number of other such requirements that you should normally observe when designing classes to be held in a collection. These are mostly concerned with overriding the default implementation of standard methods inherited from the `Object` class. The requirements are as follows.

▶ Override the `equals` method to ensure that any collection class method involving an equality test will work.

▶ Override the `toString` method to enable easy printing of the contents of the collection (for example, during debugging).

▶ Override the `hashCode` method if objects of this class are likely to be held in a collection based on a hash table, such as `HashMap` or `HashSet`.

▶ Implement the `Comparable` interface if objects of this class are likely to be used in a sorted array or sorted collection.

▶ Ensure that the `equals` method and the `hashCode` method are consistent. This means that `a.equals(b)` must imply that `a.hashCode == b.hashCode` for any two objects `a` and `b` for this class.

▶ Ensure that `compareTo` is defined consistently with the `equals` method for this class.

In most of the examples we have seen in this unit, the collections have contained `String` or `Integer` objects that already comply with these requirements. If you are using classes of your own in collections, it is your responsibility to follow the above guidelines – the default implementations in `Object` will not work properly.

SAQ 10

Which collection class, from those discussed in this unit, would you use for the following application?

A program runs across a large number of networked computers in order to identify as many prime numbers as possible. At the central server computer we wish to store these prime numbers in ascending order, so that we can print them out when necessary. Assume the prime numbers will be sent by the client computers in random order, as the client computers work sporadically on different ranges of possible prime numbers – the same number may even be sent by several computers, but we want to store it only once.

ANSWER...

We first look at the main abstract types in the Java 2 Collections Framework (Figure 11) and go through the following possibilities.

1   The data consists of individual items, not mapped pairs, so we do not need any kind of map.

2   This leaves some kind of list or set. Since we do not want to store duplicate numbers, a set seems a better choice. We have the choice of the `HashSet` or `TreeSet` implementations.

3   We want the prime numbers in ascending order, so we need a sorted set as provided by the `TreeSet` class. Class `HashSet` does not guarantee any particular order when we come to retrieve the data using an iterator.

12 Summary

This unit has described a number of topics that are concerned with the large-scale development of Java code.

First, we considered packages as a convenient means of structuring larger systems into groups of related classes. We discussed how to set up and identify your own packages and the advantages of this, such as separate 'name spaces' for program identifiers. We then looked in some detail at the Java standard packages, which provide the Java class libraries.

We listed the most important standard packages and studied the `java.util` package in more detail, as an example, and because of the fundamental role of its collection classes. We briefly outlined two simple collection classes, `ArrayList` and `HashMap`, to give an idea of various basic principles applying to all Java collection classes. This brought out the vital importance of being familiar with using the online Java API documentation.

Interfaces enable us to impart consistency and structure to the behaviour of groups of classes and give Java an alternative to multiple inheritance, without the normal problems multiple inheritance causes in other languages.

The important idea of abstract classes showed how to mirror the abstraction levels in an inheritance hierarchy.

Finally, we applied this understanding of abstract classes and interfaces to the study of the Java Collections Framework. We focused on the `LinkedList` and `HashSet` classes as representative examples. We looked at how they fit into the framework and how to use them in practice. This brought us to the very important concept of iterators and we gave examples of how to apply these across a range of collection classes.

LEARNING OUTCOMES

When you have completed this unit, you should be able to:

- ▶ use the Java API documentation to find out about Java packages and classes;
- ▶ use library classes from the standard Java packages;
- ▶ broadly understand the contents of the `java.util` package;
- ▶ use some of the important collection classes provided within the `java.util` package;
- ▶ define your own packages for structuring large programs;
- ▶ explain the role of the `Object` class in heterogeneous collections;
- ▶ explain the concept of an interface and its role in relation to multiple inheritance;
- ▶ understand the concept of an abstract class;
- ▶ use polymorphism in connection with abstract classes;
- ▶ contrast interfaces and abstract classes;
- ▶ use the `Iterator` interface defined for Java collection classes.

Concepts

The following concepts have been introduced in this unit:

abstract class, abstract method, aggregation, algorithm, API, `ArrayList`, `ArrayList` size, class library, collection class, compilation unit, composition, concrete class, concrete method, deque, `equals`, factor out (common behaviour), fully qualified name, generic, generic collection, has-a, hash table, `HashSet`, `HashMap`, heterogeneous collection, homogeneous collection, `implements`, `import`, import-on-demand, interface, is-a, iterator, Java Collections Framework, JavaDoc, key–value pair, legacy collection class, library class, linked list, `LinkedList`, list, map, multiple inheritance, name clash, object wrapper, `package`, package visibility, polymorphism, simple name, standard Java package, subpackage, tree, wild card.

Index